The Legendary History of the Cross

A SERIES OF
SIXTY-FOUR WOODCUTS
FROM A DUTCH BOOK PUBLISHED
by
VELDENER, A.D. 1483

With
An Introduction
Written and Illustrated
by
John Ashton

Preface by
S. Baring Gould, M.A.

NATAL PUBLISHING LLC
ARS LONGA, VITA BREVIS

PREFACE

THE origin of the mediæval romance of the Cross is hard to discover. It was very popular. It occurs in a good number of authors, and is depicted in a good many churches in stained glass.

I may perhaps be allowed here to repeat what I have said in my article on the Legend of the Cross, in "Myths of the Middle Ages:"—

"In the churches of the city of Troyes alone it appears in the windows of four: S. Martin-ès-Vignes, S. Pantaléon, S. Madeleine, and S. Nizier. It is frescoed along the walls of the choir of S. Croce at Florence, by the hand of Agnolo Gaddi. Pietro della Francesca also dedicated his pencil to the history of the Cross in a series of frescoes in the chapel of the Bacci, in the church of S. Francesco at Arezzo. It occurs as a predella painting among the specimens of early art at the Accademia delle Belle Arti at Venice, and is the subject of a picture by Beham, in the Munich Gallery. The Legend is told in full in the 'Vita Christi,' printed at Troyes in 1517; in the 'Legenda Aurea' of Jacques de Voragine; in a French MS. of the thirteenth century, in the British Museum. Gervase of Tilbury relates a portion of it in his 'Otia Imperalia,' quoting Peter Comestor; it appears in the 'Speculum Historiale' of Gottfried of Viterbo, in the 'Chronicon Engelhusii,' and elsewhere."

In the very curious Creation window of S. Neot's Church, Cornwall, Seth is represented putting three pips of the Tree of Life into the mouth and nostrils of dead Adam, as he buries him.

Of the popularity of the story of the Cross there can be no doubt, but its origin is involved in obscurity. It is generally possible to track most of the religious and popular folk tales and romances of the Middle Ages to their origin, which is frequently Oriental, but it is not easy to do so with the Legend of the Cross. It would rather seem that it was made up by some romancer out of all kinds of pre existing material, with no other object than to write a religious novel for pious readers, to displace the sensuous novels which were much in vogue.

We know that this was largely done after the third century, and a number of martyr legends, such as those of S. Apollinaris Syncletica, SS. Cyprian and Justina, the story of Duke Procopius, S. Euphrosyne, SS. Zosimus and Mary, SS. Theophanes and Pansemne, and many others were composed with this object. The earliest of all is undoubtedly the Clementine Recognitions, which dates from a remotely early period, and carries us into the heart of Petrine Christianity, and in which many a covert attack is made on S. Paul and his teaching. On the other hand, we know that an Asiatic priest, as Tertullian tells us, wrote a romance on "Paul and Thecla, out of love to Paul." S. Jerome says that a Pauline zealot, when convicted before his bishop of having written the romance, tried to exculpate himself by saying that he had done it out of admiration for S. Paul, but the Bishop would not accept the excuse, and deprived him. Unfortunately this romance has not come down to us, though we have another on S. Paul and his relations to Thecla, who is said to have accompanied him on his apostolic rambles, disguised in male attire.

The Greek romance literature was not wholesome reading for Christians. Some of the writers of these tales became Christian bishops, and probably devoted their facile pens to more edifying subjects than the difficulties of parted lovers.

Heliodorus, who wrote "Theagenes and Charicheia," is said to have become Bishop of Tricca, in Thessaly. Socrates, in the fifth century, in speaking of clerical celibacy, mentions the severity of the rule imposed on his clergy by this Heliodorus, "under whose name there are love-books extant, called Ethiopica, which he composed in his youth."

Achilles Tatius, author of the "Loves of Clitophon and Leucippe," is said also to have become a bishop. So also Eustathius of Thessalonica, author of the "Lives of Hysemene and Hysmenias," but this is more than doubtful.

Three things conduced to the production of a Christian romance literature in the early ages of the Church:—(1) The necessity under which the Church lay of supplying a want in human nature; (2) The need there was for producing some light wholesome literature to supply the place of the popular love-romances then largely read and circulated; (3) The fact that some bishops and converts were experienced novel writers, and therefore ready to lend their hands to some better purpose than amusing the leisure and flattering the passions of the idle and young.

Much the same conditions existed in the Middle Ages. There was an influx of sensuous literature from the East, through the Arabs of Spain and Sicily; Oriental tales easily took Western garb, in which the caliphs became kings of Christendom, and the fakirs and imauns were converted into monks and Catholic priests. To counteract these stories, collections of which may be found in Le Grand d'Aussi and Von der Hagen, and in Boccaccio, the Gesta Romanorum was drawn up, a collection of moral tales, many of them of similar Oriental parentage. But beside these short stories, or novels, were long romances, some heroic, and founded on early national traditions and ballads. To these belong the Niebelungen Lied and Noth, the Gudrun, the Heldenbuch, the cycles of Karlovingian and of Arthurian romance.

As it happens, we have two authors in the Middle Ages, living much about the same time, one intensely heathen in all his conceptions, the other as entirely Christian, each dealing with subjects from the same cycle, and the one writing in avowed opposition to the tendency of the other's book. I allude to Wolfram of Eschenbach and Gottfried of Strassburg. The latter wrote the Tristram, the former the Parzival. In Gottfried, the moral sense seems to be absolutely dead; there is no perception of the sacredness of truth, of chastity, of honour, none of religion. Wolfram is his exact converse. Wolfram gives us the history of the Grail, but he did not invent the myth of the Grail, he derived it from pre-existing material. The Grail myth is almost certainly heathen in its origin, but it has been entirely Christianised. The holy basin is that in which the Blood of Christ is preserved, and only the pure of heart can see it; but the Grail was really the great cauldron of Nature, the basin of Ceridwen, the earth goddess of the Kelts, or, among Teutonic nations, the sacrificial cauldron of Odin, in which was brewed the spirit of poesy, of the blood of Mimer. The remembrance of the mysterious vessel remained after Kelt and Teuton had become Christian, and the poets and romancists gave it a new spell of life by christening it. It was much the same with the story of the Cross. In the Teutonic North, tree worship was widely spread; the tree was sacred to Odin, who himself, according to the mysterious Havamal, hung nine nights wounded, as a sacrifice to himself, a voluntary sacrifice, in "the wind-rocked tree."

That tree was Yggdrasill, the world tree, whose roots extended to hell, and whose branches spread to heaven.

Northern mythology is full of allusion to this tree, but we have, unfortunately, little of the history of it preserved to us; we know of it only through allusions. The Christmas tree is its representative; it has been taken up out of paganism, and rooted in Christian soil, where it flourishes to the annual delight of thousands of children.

Now the mediæval romancists laid hold of this tree, as they laid hold of the Grail basin, and used it for Christian purposes. The Grail cup became the chalice of the Blood of Christ, and the Tree of Odin became the Cross of Calvary. They worked into the romance all kinds of material gathered from floating folk-tale of heathen ancestry, and they pieced in with it every scrap of allusion to a tree they could find in Scripture. It is built up of fragments taken from all kinds of old structures, put together with some skill, and built into a goodly romance; but the tracing of every stone to its original quarry has not been done by anyone as yet. The Grail myth has had many students and interpreters, but not the Cross myth. That remains to be examined, and it will doubtless prove a study rewarding the labour of investigation.

S. BARING-GOULD

THE LEGENDARY
HISTORY OF THE CROSS

THE Cross on which our Lord and Saviour suffered, would, naturally, if properly authenticated, be an object of the deepest veneration to all Christian men, be their creed, or shade of opinion what it might; but, for over 300 years it could not be found, and it was reserved for the Empress Helena in her old age (for she was 79 years old) to discover its place of concealment.[1]

Rufinus on the Invention.

That this *Invention*, or finding of the Cross was believed in, at the time, there can be no manner of doubt, for it is alluded to by St. Cyril, Patriarch of Jerusalem (A.D. 350 to 386), and by St. Ambrose. Rufinus of Aquila, a friend of St. Jerome, in his *Ecclesiastical History*, gives an account of its finding, in the following words: "About the same time, Helena, the mother of Constantine, a woman of incomparable faith, whose sincere piety was equaled by her rare munificence, warned by celestial visions, went to Jerusalem, and inquired of the inhabitants where was the place where the Divine Body had been affixed and hung on a gibbet. This place was difficult to find, for the persecutors of old had raised a statue to Venus,[2] in order that the Christians who might wish to adore Christ in that place, should appear to address their homage to the goddess; and thus it was little frequented, and almost forgotten. After clearing away the

---

[1] *A.D. 326.*

[2] *Hadrian is said to have done this.*

profane objects which defiled it, and the rubbish that was there heaped up, she found three crosses placed in confusion. But the joy which this discovery caused her was tempered by the impossibility of distinguishing to whom each of them had belonged. There, also, was found the title written by Pilate in Greek, Latin, and Hebrew characters; but still there was nothing to indicate sufficiently clearly the Cross of our Lord. This uncertainty of man was settled by the testimony of heaven." And then follows the story of the dead woman being raised to life.

Other Authorities.

Not only did Rufinus write thus, but Socrates, Theodoret, and Sozomen, all of whom lived within a century after the *Invention*, tell the same story, so that it must have been of current belief.

Punishment of the Cross.

The punishment of the Cross was a very ordinary one, and of far wider extent than many are aware. It was common among the Scythians, the Greeks, the Carthaginians, the Germans, and the Romans, who, however, principally applied it to their slaves, and rarely crucified free men, unless they were robbers or assassins.

Alexander the Great, after taking the city of Tyre, caused two thousand inhabitants to be crucified.

Punishment of the Cross.

Flavius Josephus relates, in his *Antiquities of the Jews*, that Alexander, the King of the Jews, on the capture of the town of Betoma, ordered eight hundred of the inhabitants to suffer the death of the Cross, and their wives and children to be massacred before their eyes, whilst they were still alive.

Augustus, after the Sicilian War, crucified six thousand slaves who had not been claimed by their masters.

Tiberius crucified the priests of Isis, and destroyed their temple.

Titus, during the siege of Jerusalem, crucified all those unfortunates who, to the number of five or six hundred daily, fled from the city to escape the famine; and so numerous were these executions, that crosses were wanting, and the land all about seemed like a hideous forest.

The different sorts of Crosses.

These instances are sufficient to show that death by crucifixion was a common punishment; but, singularly enough, the shape of the Cross has never been satisfactorily settled; practically, the question lies between the *Crux capitata*, or *immissa*, which is the ordinary form of the Latin Cross, and the *Crux ansata*, or *commissa*, frequently called the *Tau* Cross, from the Greek letter T. The *Tau*-shaped Cross is, undoubtedly, to be met with most frequently in the older representations; and the more ancient authorities, such as Tertullian, St. Jerome, St. Paulinus, Sozomen, and Rufinus, are of opinion that this was the shape of the Cross. After the fifteenth century, our Lord is rarely depicted on the *Crux commissa*, it being reserved for the two thieves.

Antiquity of the Tau Cross.

M. Adolphe Napoleon Didron, in his *Iconographie Chretienne*, gives a few illustrations of the antiquity of the *Tau* Cross: "The Cross is our crucified Lord in person; 'Where the Cross is, there is the martyr,' says St. Paulinus. Consequently it works miracles, as does Jesus Himself: and the list of wonders operated by its power is in truth immense. By the simple sign of the Cross traced upon the forehead or the breast, men have been delivered from the most imminent danger. It has constantly put demons to flight, protected the virginity of women, and the faith of believers; it has restored men to life, or health, inspired them with hope or resignation.

"Such is the virtue of the Cross, that a mere allusion to that sacred sign, made even in the Old Testament, and long before the existence of the Cross, saved the youthful Isaac from death, redeemed from destruction an entire people whose houses were marked by that symbol, healed the envenomed bites of those who looked at the serpent raised in the form of a *Tau* upon a pole. It called back the soul into the dead body of the son of that poor widow who had given bread to the prophet.

The Tau Cross.

"A beautiful painted window, belonging to the thirteenth century, in the Cathedral of Bourges, has a representation of Isaac bearing on his shoulders the wood that was to be used in his sacrifice, arranged in the form of a Cross; the Hebrews, too, marked the lintel of their dwellings with the blood of the Paschal lamb, in the form of a *Tau* or Cross without a summit. The widow of Sarepta picked up and held crosswise two pieces of wood, with which she intended to bake her bread. These figures, to which others also may be added, serve to exalt the triumph of the Cross, and seem to flow from a grand central picture which forms their source, and exhibits Jesus expiring on the Cross. It is from that real Cross indeed, bearing the Saviour, that these subjects from the Old Testament derive all their virtue."

Wood of the Cross - Cross made of pine.

The wood of which it was made is as unsettled as its shape. The Venerable Bede says that our Lord's Cross was made of four kinds of wood: the inscription of box, the upright beam of cypress, the transverse of cedar, and the lower part of pine. John Cantacuméne avers that only three woods were employed: the upright, cedar; the transverse, pine; and the head in cypress. Others say that the upright was cypress, the transverse in palm, and the head in olive; or cedar, cypress, and olive. Most authorities seem to concur that it was made of several woods, but there is a legend that it was made from the aspen tree, whose leaves still tremble at the awful use the tree was put to; whilst that veritable traveller, Sir John Maundeville, says: "And also in Iherusalem toward the Weast is a fayre church where the tree grew of the which the Crosse was made." Lipsius says that it was made of but one wood, and that was oak; but M. Rohault de Fleury (to whose wonderful and comprehensive work, *Mémoire sur les Instruments de la Passion de notre Sauveur Jesus Christ*, I am deeply indebted, says, "M. Decaisne, member of the Institut, and M. Pietro Savi, professor at the University of Pisa, have shewn me by the microscope that the pieces in the Church of the Holy Cross of Jerusalem at Rome, in the Cathedral at Pisa, in the Duomo at Florence, and in

Notre Dame at Paris, were of *pine*." And he adds, in a footnote, "Independently of the experiments which M. Savi kindly made in my presence, he wrote me the results of other observations, which tended to confirm."

Starting with the Invention of the Holy Cross, the loving, but fervid, imaginations of the faithful soon wove round it a covering of imagery, as we have just seen in the case of the several woods of the Cross, and the sacred tree became the subject of a legend (for so it always was only meant to be), which was incorporated in the *Legenda Aurea Sanctorum*, or *Golden Legend of the Saints*, of Jacobus de Voragine, a collection of legends connected with the services of the Church. This book was exceedingly popular, and, when Caxton set up his printing-press at Westminster, he produced a translation, the history of which he quaintly tells us in a preface.[3]

Caxton's Golden Legend

As this Golden Legend is the standard authority on the subject, and as it will much assist the intelligent appreciation of the wood-blocks, I reproduce it, premising that I have used throughout the first edition, 20 Nov., 1483:—

But alle the dayes of adam lyvynge here in erthe amounte

---

[3] "And for as moche as this sayd worke was grete & over chargeable to me taccomplisshe, I feryd me in the begynnynge of the translacion to have contynued it / bycause of the longe tyme of the translacion / & also in thenpryntyng of ye same and in maner halfe desperate to have accomplissd it / was in purpose to have lefte it / after that I had begonne to translate it / & to have layed it aparte ne had it be(en) at thynstance & requeste of the puyssant noble & vertuous erle my lord wyllyam erle of arondel / whych desyred me to procede & contynue the said werke / & promysed me to take a resonable quantyte of them when they were acheyeued & accomplisshed / and sente to me a worshypful gentylman a servaunt of his named John Stanney which solycyted me in my Lordes name that I shold in no wyse leve it but accomplisshe it promysyng that my sayd lord shold duringe my lyf geve & graunt to me a yeroly fee / that is to wete a bucke in sommer / & a doo in Wynter / with whiche fee I holde me wel contente." &c.

to the somme of ixCxxx⁴ yere / And in thende of his lyf whan

---

⁴ *Length of Adam's life.* This apparently long life of Adam is admitted on all hands, even in the Revised Version of the Bible. The Talmud says that God promised him one thousand years of life, and it is recorded that he begat Seth when he was a hundred and thirty years old. On this the Talmud (*Eruvin*, fol. 18, col. 2) has the following comment: "Rav Yirmyah ben Elazer said: All those years, which Adam spent in alienation from God, he begat evil spirits, demons, and fairies; for it is said, 'And Adam was an hundred and thirty years, and begat a son in his own likeness, after his image'; consequently, before that time, he begat after another image."

This term of one hundred and thirty years seems to have been a period in Adam's existence, for we again find (*Eruvin*, fol. 18 b.): "Adam was a Chasid, or great saint, when he observed that the decree of death was occasioned by him; he *fasted* a hundred and thirty years, and all this time he abstained from intercourse with his wife."

Talmud legends respecting Adam's length of life.

There is a Talmudical tradition that God showed the future to Adam (Avoth d'Rab. Nathan, chap. 31): "The Holy One—blessed be He!—shewed unto Adam each generation, and its preachers, its guardians, its leaders, its prophets, its heroes, its sinners, and its saints, saying, 'In such and such a generation such and such a *King* shall reign, in such and such a generation such and such a wife man shall teach.'" This is amplified in Midrash Yalkut (fol. 12), where it is said that God showed Adam all future generations of men, with their leaders, learned and literary men, and there he observed that David was credited with only three hours of life, and he said, "Lord and Creator of the world, is this unalterable?" "Such was my first intention," was the reply. "How many years have I to live?" asked Adam. "One thousand." Then Adam said, "I will lend him some of my years." And a document was drawn up whereby Adam transferred seventy years of his life to David.

S. Baring-Gould, in his legends of *Old Testament Characters*, vol i. p. 77, referring to a Mussulman legend, says: "Finally, when Adam reached his nine hundred and thirtieth year, the Angel of Death appeared under the form of a goat, and ran between his legs.

"Adam recoiled with horror, and exclaimed, 'God has given me one thousand years; wherefore comest thou now?'

"'What!' exclaimed the Angel of Death, 'hast thou not given seventy years of thy life to the prophet David?'

"Adam stoutly denied that he had done so. Then the Angel of Death drew the document of transfer from out of his beard, and

Of thynuencyon of tholy crosse / and first of thys worde Inuencion

he shold dye / it is said but of none auctoryte / that he sente Seth his sone in to paradys for to fetch the oyle of mercy / where he receyuyde certayn graynes of the fruyt of the tree of mercy by an angel / And whan he come agayn / he fonde his fader adam yet alyve and told hym what he had don. And thenne Adam lawhed[5] first / and then deyed / and thenne he leyed the greynes or kernellis under his faders tonge and buryed hym / in the vale of ebron / and out of his mouth grewe thre trees of the thre graynes / of which the crosse that our lord suffred his passion on / was made by vertue of which he gate[6] very mercy and was brought out of darknes in to veray light of heven / to the whiche he brynge us that lyveth and regneth god world with oute ende.

The Invencion[7] of the holy crosse is said bycause that this day the holy crosse was founden / for to fore[8] it was founden

presented it to Adam, who could no longer refuse to go."

[5] *Laughed or smiled.*

[6] *Obtained true mercy.*

[7] The Festival of the Invention, or finding of the Cross, is kept in the Roman and English Churches on May 3.

[8] *Of old.*

of seth in paradyse terestre / lyke as hit shal be sayd here after / and also it was founden of salamon in the mounte of lybane and of the quene of saba / in the temple of salamon / And of the Iewes in the water of pyscyne[9]/ And on thys day it was founden of Helayne in the mounte of Calvarye/.

OF THE HOLY CROSSE

The holy crosse was founden two hondred yere after the resurrexyon of our lord / It is redde in the gospel of nychodemus[10]/ that whan adam wexyd seck / Seth hys sone wente to the gate of paradyse terestre, for to gete the oyle of mercy for to enoynte wythal hys faders body / Thenne apperyd to hym saynt mychel thaungel and sayd to hym / travayle not the in vayne / for thys oyle / for thou mayst not

---

[9] Piscina, a fish-pond: *Lat.* In this instance it is supposed to be the Pool of Bethesda.

[10] Nicodemus, chap. 14:— *v.* 1. But when the first man our father Adam heard these things, that Jesus was baptized in Jordan, he called out to his son Seth, and said, *v.* 2. Declare to your sons, the patriarchs and prophets, all those things which thou didst hear from Michael the Archangel, when I sent thee to the gates of Paradise to entreat God that he would anoint my head when I was sick. *v.* 3 Then Seth, coming near to the patriarchs and prophets, said: I, Seth, when I was praying to God at the gates of Paradise, beheld the angel of the Lord, Michael, appear unto me, saying, I am sent unto thee from the Lord; I am appointed to preside over human bodies. *v.* 4. I tell thee, Seth, do not pray to God in tears, and entreat him for the oil of the tree of mercy, wherewith to anoint thy father Adam for his headache; *v.* 5. Because thou canst not by any means obtain it till the last day and times, namely, till five thousand and five hundred years be past. *v.* 6. Then will Christ, the most merciful Son of God, come on earth to raise again the human body of Adam, and at the same time to raise the bodies of the dead, and when he cometh he will be baptized in Jordan; *v.* 7. Then with the oil of his mercy he will anoint all those that believe on him; and the oil of his mercy will continue to future generations, for those who shall be born of the water and the Holy Ghost unto eternal life. *v.* 8. And when at that time the most merciful Son of God, Christ Jesus, shall come down on earth, he will introduce our father Adam into Paradise, to the tree of mercy. *v.* 9. When all the patriarchs and prophets heard all these things from Seth, they rejoiced more.

---

have it till fyve thousand and fyve hondred yere been passed
/ how be it that fro Adam unto the passyon of our lord were
but five ℳℭ and xxxiiij yere / In another place it is redde that
the aungel broughte hym a braunche / and commaunded hym
to plante it in the mounte of lybanye Yet fynde we in another
place / that he gafe to hym of the tree that Adam ete of / And
sayd to hym that whan that bare fruyte he should be
guarisshed[11] and alle hoole[12]/. whan seth came ageyn he
founde his fader deed / and planted this tree upon his grave /
And it endured there un to the tyme of Salomon / and bycause
he sawe that it was fayre, he dyd[13] doo hewe it doun / and
sette it in his hows named saltus / and whan the quene of saba
came to vysyte Salamon / She worshypped this tre bycause
she sayd the savyour of alle the world shold be hanged there
on / by whome the royame[14] of the Iewes that be defaced and
seace.[15] Salomon for this cause made hit to be taken up / &
dolven[16] depe in the grounde. Now it happed after that they
of Ierusalem (dyd do make a grete pytte for a pyscyne[17]/
where at the mynysters of the temple sholde wesshe theyre
bestys / that they shold sacrefyse / and there founde thys tre /
and thys pyscyne had suche vertue, that the aungels
descended and mevyd the water / and the first seke man that
descendyd in to the water after the mevyng / was made hole
of what somever sekenesse he was seek of. And whan the
tyme approched of the passyon of our lord / thys tree aroos
out of the water and floted above the water / And of this pyece
of tymbre made the Iewes the crosse of our lord / Thenne after
this hystorye / the crosse by which we been saved / came of
the tree by whiche we were dampned. And the water of that
pyscyne had not his vertue onely of the aungel / but of the
tre/. With this tre wherof the crosse was maad / there was a
tree that went over thwarte / on whiche the armes of our lord
were nayled/. And another pyece above which was the table

---

[11] *Cured: French, guerir, to heal.*
[12] *Whole.*
[13] *Did so—caused to be: words of frequent occurrence.*
[14] *Kingdom: French, royaume.*
[15] *Cease.*
[16] *Dug, p. part. of delve.*
[17] *Pond.*

/ wherin the tytle was wryten / and another pyece wherein the sokette or mortys was maad that the body of the crosse stood in soo that there were foure manere of trees / That is of palme of cypres / of cedre and of olyve. So eche of thyse foure pyeces was of one of those trees/. This blessed crosse was put in the erthe and hyd by the space of on hondred yere and more / But the moder of themperour which was named helayne[18] which founde it in thys manere / For Constantyn came wyth a grete multytude of barbaryns nygh unto the ryver of the dunoe / whyche wold have goon over for to have destroyed alle the contree / And whan constantyn had assembled his hoost / He went and sette them ageynst that other partye / But as sone as he began to passe the ryver / he was moche aferde / by cause he shold on the morne have batayle / and in the

---

[18] Alban Butler, in *The Lives of the Fathers, Martyrs, and other Principal Saints*, denies that St. Helena was an Innholder (*Stabularia*) in Bithynia, when Constantius married her, and says: "We are assured by the unanimous tradition of our English historians that this holy empress was a native of our island. William of Malmesbury, the principal historian of the ancient state of our country after Bede, and before him, the Saxon author of the life of St. Helen, in 970, quoted by Usher, expressly say that Constantine was a Briton by birth." Leland, in his *Commentarii de Scriptoribus Britannicis*, says that St. Helena was the only daughter of King Coilus, the King Cöol who first built walls round Colchester, and the English Church has generally recognised her British origin. Her festival is kept on August 18.

When her husband, Constantine Chlorus, entered into an arrangement with Diocletian, by which he had the countries this side the Alps, namely, Gaul and Britain, he was obliged, as part of the bargain, to divorce St. Helena, and marry Theodora, the daughter-in-law of Maximinianus. According to Eusebius, she was not converted to Christianity at the same time as her son Constantine, who, when he came to the throne, paid her the greatest deference, and gave her the title of Augusta, or empress. After the Council of Nice, in 325, he wrote to Macarius, Bishop of Jerusalem, concerning the building of a splendid church upon Mount Calvary, and St. Helena, although she was then 79 years of age, undertook to see it carried out.

It was then that the reputed Invention of the Cross, together with the nails, took place, and she soon afterwards died, but the exact year is uncertain, some authorities giving A.D. 326, others 328.

nyght as he slepte in his bedde / an aungel awoke hym / and shewed to hym the sygne of the crosse in heven / and sayd to hym / Beholde on hye on heven/. Thanne sawe he the crosse made of ryght clere lyght / & was wryten there upon wyth lettres of golde / In this sygne thou shalte over come the batayle/ Thenne was he alle comforted of thys vysion / And on the morne / he put in his banere the Crosse[19]/ and made it to be borne tofore hym and his hoost / And after smote in the hoost of his enemyes / and slewe and chaced grete plente / After thys he dyd doo[20] calle the bysshoppes of the ydolles / and demaunded them to what god the sygne of the crosse apperteyned. And whan they coude not answere / some cristen men that were there tolde to hym the mysterye of the crosse / and enformed hym in the faythe of the trynyte / Thenne anone he bylevyd parfytly (in) god / and dyd do baptyse hym / and after, it happed that constantyn his sone remembred the vyctorye of his fader / Sente to helayn his modre for to fynde the holy crosse / Thenne helayne wente in to Iherusalem / and dyd doo assemble all the wyse men of the contre / and whan they were assembled / they wold fayn knowe wherfore they were called / Thenne one Iudas sayd to them / I wote[21] wel that she wyl knowe of us where the crosse of Ihesu criste was leyed / but beware you al that none of you tell hyr / for I wote wel then shall our lawe be destroyed / For zacheus my olde[22] fader sayde to symon my fader / And my fader sayde to me at his dethe / be wel ware / that for no tormente that ye may suffre / telle not where the crosse of

Ihesu criste was leyde / for after that hit shal be founden / the Iewes shal reygne no mour / But the cristen men that worshypped the

---

[19] *The Læbarum, or Sacred Banner of Constantine.*

[20] *Caused to be called together.*

[21] *Know.*

[22] *Grandfather.*

crosse shal then reygne / And verayly this Ihesus was the sone of god. Then demaunded I my fader / wherfore had they hanged hym on the crosse sythe it was knowen that he was the sone of god / thenne he sayd to me fayre sone I never accorded thereto / But gayn said it alwaye / But the Pharisees dyd it bycause he repreyvd theyr vyces / but he aroos on the thyrd day / and his dysciples seeing / he ascended in to heven / Thenne by cause that Stephen thy broder belevyd in him / the Iewes stoned hym to dethe.

Then when Iudas had sayd theyse wordes to his selawes / they answerd we never herde of suche thynges / never the lesse kepe the wel if the quene demaunde the therof / that thou say no thynge to hyr / Whan the quene had called them / and demaunded them the place where our lord Ihesu criste had been crucefyed/ they wold never tell her nor ensygne[23] her /. Then commaunded she to brenne[24] them alle/. But then they doubted and were aferde / & delyvered Iudas to hyr and sayd / lady thys man is the sone of a prophete and of a juste man / and knoweth right wel the lawe / & can telle to you al thynge that ye shal demaunde hym/.

Thenne the quene lete al the other goo, and reteyned Iudas without moo[25]/. Thenne she shewed to hym his life & dethe & bade hym chese whyche he wold. Shewe to me sayd she the place named golgota where our lord was crucefyed / by cause and to the end that we may fynde the crosse/. Thenne sayd Iudas, it is two hondred yere passed & more / & I was not thenne yet borne. Thenne sayd to hym the lady / by him that was crucyfyed / I shal make the perisse for hungre/ yf thou telle not to me the trouthe.

Thenne made she hym to be caste into a drye pytte / and there tormented hym by hungre / and evyl reste / whan he had been seuen dayes in that pytte / thenne sayd he yf I myght be drawen out / he shold say the trouthe / Thenne he was drawen out / and when he came to the place / anone the erthe moevyd and a fume of grete swettnesse was felte in suche wyse that Iudas smote his hondes togyder for ioye / and sayd / in trouthe

---

[23] *Inform.*
[24] *Burn.*
[25] *More ado.*

Ihesu criste thou art the savyour of the worlde.

It was so that adryan the Emperour had doo make in the same place where the crosse laye a temple of a goddesse by cause that all they that come in that place shold adoure that goddesse/. But the quene did doo destroy the temple / Thenne Iudas made hym redy and began to dygge / and whan he came to xx paas[26] depe / he fonde three crosses and broughte them to the quene / And bycause he knewe not whiche was the crosse of our lord / he leyed them in the myddel of the cyte / and abode the demonstraunce of god / and aboute the houre of none / there was the corps of a yonge man brought to be buryed / Iudas reteyned the byere / and layed upon hit one of the crosses / and after the second / and whan he leyed on hit the third / anone the body that was dede came ageyn to lyf/.

Thenne cryed the devyll in the eyre Iudas what hast thou doon / thou hast doon the contrarye that thother Iudas dyd/. For by hym I have wonne many sowles / and by the I shal lose many / by hym I reygned on the peple / And by the I have lost my royame / never the lesse I shal yelde to the this bountee/. For I shal send one that shal punysshe the / and that was accomplysshed by Iulian the apostata / which tormented hym afterward whan he was bysshop of Iherusalem / and whan Iudas herde hym he cursed the devyl and sayd to hym / Ihesu cryste dampne the in fyre pardurable[27]/. After this Iudas was baptyzed and was named quyryache[28]/. And after was made bysshop of Iherusalem/. Whan helayn had the crosse of Ihesu criste / and saw she had not the nayles / Thenne he dyd dygge in therthe so longe / that he founde them shynyng as golde/. thenne bare he them to the quene / and anone as she sawe them she worshypped them wyth grete reverence/.

Thenne gafe saynt helayn a part of the crosse to hir sone / And that other parte she lefte in Iherusalem closyd in golde / sylver and precious stones/.

And hyr sone bare the nayles to themperour / And the emperour dyd do sette them in hys brydel and in hys helme

---

[26] *Twenty Paces.*

[27] *Everlasting.*

[28] Other accounts say the Crosses were found by Macarius, then Bishop of Jerusalem.

whan he wente to batayle/. This referreth Eusebe whiche was bysshop of Cezayr[29]/ how be it that other say otherwyse/. Now it happed that Iulyan the appostate dyd doo[30] slee quyriache that was bysshop of Iherusalem / by cause he had founde the crosse / for he hated hit soo mooche / that where somever he founde the crosse / he dyd hit to be destroyed / For whan he wente in batayle ageynste them of perse / he sente and commaunded quyriache to make sacrefyse to thydolles / and whan he wold not doo hit / he dyd do smyte of his right honde / and sayd wyth this honde hast thou wryten many letters / by whyche thou repellyd moche folke fro doynge sacrefyse to our goddes/.

Quyriache sayd thou wood hounde[31] thou hist doon to me grete prouffyte / For thou hast cut of the hande / wyth whiche I have many tymes wreton to the synagoges that they shold not byleve in Ihesu criste / and now sythe[32] I am cristen / thou hast taken from me that whiche noyed me / thenne dyd Iulyan do melte leed, and caste it in his mowthe / and after dyd doo brynge a bedde of yron / and made quyriache to be layed and stratched theron / and after leyed under brennyng cooles / and threwe therein grece and salte / for to torment hym the more / and whan quyriache moved not / Iulyan themperour said to hym / outher thou shalt sacrefyse (to) our goddes / or thou shalt say at the leste thou art not cristen/. And whan he sawe he wolde not do never neyther / he dyd doo make a depe pytte ful of serpentes and venemous bestys / and caste hym therein / & whan he entred / anone the serpentes were al deed/. Thenne Iulyan put hym in a cawdron ful of boylyng oyle / and whan he shold entre in to hit / he blessyd it & sayd / Fayre lord torne thys bane[33] to baptysm of marterdom / Thenne was Iulyan moche angry / and commaunded that he should be ryven thorough his herte with a swerde / and in this manere he fynysshed his lyff.

The vertue of the crosse is declared to us by many

---

[29] *Eusebius, Bishop of Cesarœa.*
[30] *Killed.*
[31] *Mad dog.*
[32] *Since.*
[33] *Turn this evil*

miracles / For it happed on a tyme that one enchantour had dysceyved a notarye / and brought hym to a place / where he had assembled a grete companye of devylles / and promysed to hym to have muche rychesse / and whan he came there / he saw one persone blacke syttynge on a grete chayer / And all aboute hym al ful of horyble people and blacke whiche had speres and swerdes / Thenne demaunded thys grete devyll of the enchantour / who was that clerke / thenchantour sayd to hym / Syr he is oures / thenne sayd the devyl to hym yf thou wylte worshyp me and be my servaunte / and denye Ihesu cryste / thou shalt sytte on my right syde / The clerke anone blessyd hym wyth the sygne of the crosse / and sayd that he was the servaunte of Ihesu criste / his savyour / And anone as he had made the crosse / that grete multitude of devylles vanysshed aweye. It happed that this notarye after this on a tyme entryd with hys lord in the chyrche of saynt sophye / & knelyd doun on his knees to fore the ymage of the crucyfyxe / the which crucifyxe as it semed loked moche openly and sharpelye on hym/. Thenne his lord made hym to go aparte on another syde / and alleweye the crucifixe torned his eyen toward hym/. Thenne he made hym goo on the lefte syde / and yet the crucifixe loked on hym / Thenne was the lord moche admerveyled / and charged hym & commaunded hym that he shold telle hym wherof he had so deserved that the crucifyxe so behelde and loked on hym / Thenne sayde the notarye that he coude not remembre hym of no good thynge that he had doon / saufe that one tyme he wold not renye nor forsake the crucifixe tofore the devyl/.

Thenne late us so blesse us with the sygne of the blessyd crosse that we may therby be kepte fro the power of our ghoostly and dedely enemye the devyl / and by the glorious passyon that our saveour Ihesu cryst suffred on the crosse after this lyf we may come to his everlastyng blysse amen/.

Thus endeth thynvencion of the holy crosse.

Exaltation of the holy Crosse[34] is sayd / bycause that on this daye the hooly crosse & faythe were gretely enhaunced/. And it is to be understonden that tofore the passion of our lord Ihesu cryste / the tree of the crosse was a tree of fylthe / For the crosses were made of vyle trees, & of trees without fruyte / For al that was planted on the Mount of Calvarye bare no fruyt. It was a fowle place / for hit was the place of torment of thevys / It was derke / for it was in a derke place and without any beaute / It was the tree of deth / for men were put there to dethe / It was also the tree of stenche / for it was planted amonge the caroynes[35]/ & after the passyon the Crosse was moche enhaunced / For the Vylte[36] was transported into preciousyte / Of the whiche the blessyd saynt Andrewe sayth / O precious holy Crosse god save

Here foloweth the Exaltacion of the holy Crosse

the / his bareynes was torned into fruyte / as it is sayd in the Cantyques / I shall ascende up in to a palme tree / et cetera / His ignobylyte or unworthynes was tourned into sublymyte and heyght / The Crosse that was tormente of thevys is now

---

[34] *The Roman and English Churches celebrate this Festival on February 14.*
[35] *Carrion.*
[36] *Vileness.*

born in the front of themperours / his derkenes is torned into lyght and clerenesse/ wherof Chrysostom sayth the Crosse and the Woundes shall be more shynyng than the rayes of the Sonne at the jugement / his deth is converted into perdurabylyte of lyf / whereof it is sayd in the preface / that fro hens the lyf resourded[37]/ and the stenche is torned into swetenes / canticorum /. This exaltacion of the hooly crosse is solempnysed and halowed solempnly of the Chirche / For the faythe is in hit moche enhaunced /.

For the yere of oure lord five honderd & xx / our lord suffred his people moche to be tormentyd by the cruelte of the paynyms / And Cosdroe[38] Kynge of the Perceens subdued to his empyre all the Royaumes of the world / And he cam into Iherusalem and was aferd and a dred of the sepulcre of our lord & retorned / but he bare with hym the parte of the hooly Crosse / that saynte Helene had left ther. And then he wold be worshiped of alle the peple / as a god / & dyd do make a tour of gold and of sylver wherein precious stones shone / and made therein the ymages of the sonne and of the mone and of the sterres / and made that by subtyle conduytes water to be hydde / and to come doune in the maner of rayne / And in the laste stage he made horses to draw charyotes round aboute lyke as they had mevyd the toure / and made it to seme as it had thondred / and delyvered his Royaume to his sone. And thus this cursyd man abode in this Temple / and dyd doo sette the crosse of our lord by hym and commaunded that he shold be callyd god of alle the peple / And as it is redde in libro de mitrali[39] officio the said Cosdroe resydent in his trone as a fader / sette the tree of the Crosse on his ryght syde in stede of the sonne / and a cock in the lyft syde in stede of the hooly ghoost / & commaunded / that he shold be called fader /. And then Heracle[40] themperour assembled a grete hoost / and cam for to fyght wyth the sonne of Cosdroe by

---

[37] *Resourced or replenished.*

[38] *Chosroes II., who reigned in the seventh Century.*

[39] The book of the office of Mithras or Mithra, the Sun, worshipped by the Persians.

[40] Heraclius, Emperor of the East, who from A.D. 622 to 627 fought Chosroes II., defeated him, and concluded peace.

the ryver of danubie / & thenne hit pleasyd to eyther prynce / that eche of them shold fyght one ageynste that other upon the brydge / & he that shold vaynquysshe & overcome his adversarye sholde be prynce of thempyre withoute hurtyng eyther of bothe hostes / & so hit was ordeyned & sworn / & that who somever shold helpe his prynce shold have forthwith his legges & armes cut of / & to be plonged / & cast in to the Ryver.

And then Heracle commaunded hym all to god and to the hooly crosse wyth all the devocion that he myght. And thenne they fought longe / And at the last our lord gaf the vyctory to Heracle and subdued hym to his empyre / The hoost that was contrary / and alle the peple of Cosdroe obeyed them to the Crysten faythe / and receyved the hooly baptysme / And Cosdroe knew not the end of the batayll / For he was adoured and worshiped of alle the peple as a god / so that no man durst say nay to him / And thenne Heracle came to hym / and fonde hym syttinge in his syege[41] of golde / and sayd to hym / For as moche as after the manere thou hast honoured the Tree of the Crosse / yf thou wyld receyve baptym and the faythe of Ihesu Cryst / I shal gete it to the / and yet shalt thow holde thy crowne and Royamme with lytel hostages / And I shall lete the have thy lyf / and yf thou wylt not / I shall flee the wyth my swerde / and shalle smyte of thyne heed / and whanne he wold not accorde therto / he did anon do smyte of his hede / and commanded that he shold be buryed / by cause he had be(en) a Kynge /. And he fonde with hym one his sone of the age of ten yere / whome he dyd doo baptyse and lyft hym fro the fonte / and left to hym the Royaume of his fader / and then he dyd doo breke that Toure / And gaf the sylver to them of his hooste / and gaf the gold and precious stones for to repayre the chirches that the tyraunt had destroyed / and tooke the hoole crosse / and brought it ageyne to Ierusalem / and as he descended from the mount of Olyvete / and wold have entryd by the gate by whiche our savyour wente to his passyon on horsbacke adourned as a Kynge / sodenly the stones of the gates descended / and ioyned them togyder in

---

[41] *Throne, or seat; French, siège.*

the gate like a wall & all the peple was abashed[42]/ and thenne
the Aungel of oure lord appyeryd upon the gate holdyng the
signe of the signe (*sic*) of the Crosse in his honde / and sayd
/ Whanne the Kynge of heven went to his passion by this gate
/ he was not arayed like a Kynge / ne on horsbake / but cam
humbly upon an asse / in shewynge thexample of humylite
which he left to them that honoure hym. And when this was
sayd / he departed and vanysshed aweye / Thenne
th'emperour took of his hosen and shone[43] himself in
wepynge / and despollyed hymselfe of alle his clothes in to
his sherte / and tooke the crosse of oure lord / and bare it
moche humbly into the gate / and anone the hardnes of the
stones felte the celestyalle commaundement / and remeved
anone / and opened and gaf entree unto them that entred /
Thenne the sweete odour that was felt that day whanne the
hooly Crosse was taken fro the Toure of Cosdroe / and was
brought ageyne to Iherusalem fro so ferre countre / and so
grete space of londe retourned in to Iherusalem in that
moment / and replenysshed it with al swetncs / Thenne the
ryght devoute Kyng beganne to saye the praysynges of the
Crosse in this wyse / O Crux splendydior / et cetera / O
Crosse more shynynge than alle the Sterres / honoured of the
world / right holy / and moche amyable to alle men / whiche
only were worthy to bere the raunson of the world Swete tree
/ Swete nayles / Swete yron / Swete spere berynge the swete
burthens / Save thou this present company / that is this daye
assembled in thy lawe and praysynges /. And thus was the
precious tree of the Crosse re establysshed in his place / and
the auncient myracles renewed /. For a dede man was reysed
to lyf / and foure men taken with the palsey were cured and
heled / ℔ lepres were made clene / and fyften blynde receyved
theyr syghte ageyn / Devylles were put out of men / and
moche peple / and many / were delyvered of dyverse sekenes
and maladyes /. Thenne themperour dyd doo repayre the
Chirches / and gaf to them grete geftes / And after retorned
home to his Empyre / And hit is said in the Cronycles that this
was done otherwise / For they say that whanne Cosdroe

---

[42] *Astonished.*

[43] *Shoen—shoes.*

hadde taken many Royammes / he took Iherusalem / and Zacharye the patriarke / and bare aweye the tree of the Crosse / And as Heracle wold make pees with hym / the Kyng Cosdroe swore a grete othe / that he wold never make pees with Crysten men and Romayns / yf they denyed not hym that was crucyfyed / and adoured the sonne /. And thenne Heracle / whiche was armed wythe faythe / brought his hooste ageynst hym / and destroyed and wasted the Persyens with many batayles that he made to them / and made Cosdroe to flee unto the Cyte of thelyfonte /. And atte the laste Cosdroe hadde the flyxe in his bely / And wolde therefore crowne his sone Kynge / which was named Mendasa /. And whenne Syroys his oldest sone herde thereof he made alyance with Heracle / And pursewed his fader with his noble peple / and set hym in bondes / And susteyned him with breede of trybulacion / and with water of anguysshe / And atte last he made to shote arowes at him bycause he wold not bileve in god & so deyde / & after this thynge he sente to Heracle the patriarke the tree of the Crosse and all the prysoners / And Heracle bare into Iherusalem the precious tree of the Crosse /. And thus it is redde in many Cronycles also/. Sybyle sayth thus of the tre of the Crosse / that the blessyd tree of the Crosse was thre tymes with the paynyms / as it is sayd in thystorie trypertyte O thryse blessyd tree on whiche god was stratched / This peradventure is sayd for the lyf of Nature / of grace / and of glorye / which cam of the crosse /. At Constantynople a Iewe entyred in to the chirche of seynt sophye / and consydered that he was there allone / and sawe an ymage of Ihesu cryste / and tooke his swerde and smote thymage in the throte / and anone the bloode guysshed oute / and sprange in the face and on the hide of the Iewe / And he thenne was aferd and took thymage / and cast it into a pytte / and anone fledde awey /. And it happed that a Crysten man mett hym / and sawe hym al blody / and sayd to hym / fro whens comest thou / thou hast slayne soume man / And he sayd I have not / the crysten man sayd Veryly thou has commysed somme homycyde / for thou art all besprongen[44] with the blood. And the Jewe said / Veryly the god of Crysten men is grete and the faythe of hym

---

[44] *Besprinkled.*

---

is ferme and approved in all thynges / I have smyten no man / but I have smyten thymage of Ihesu Cryste / and anone yssued blood of his throte /. And thenne the Jewe brought the Crysten man to the pytte / and then they drewe oute that hooly ymage /. And yet is sene on this daye the wounde in the throte of thymage / And the Iewe anone bycam a good Crysten man, & was baptysed / In Syre in the cyte of baruth there was a cristen man / which had hyred an hous for a yere / & he had set thymage of the crucifixe by his bedde to whiche he made dayly his prayers and said his devocions / & at the yeres ende he remeved and tooke another hous / & forgate & lefte thymage behynde hym / and it happed that a Iewe hyred that same hows / & on a daye he had another Iewe one of his neyghbours to dyne / & as they were at mete it happed hym that was boden[45] in lookyng on the walle to espye this ymage whiche was fyxed to the walle and beganne to grenne at it for despyte / and ageynst hym that bad hym / & also thretned & menaced hym bycause he durst kepe in his hous thymage of Ihesu of nazareth / & that other Iewe swarc as moche as he myght / that he had never sene it / ne knewe not that it was there / & thenne the Iewe fayned as he had been peasyd[46]. / & after went strayt to the prynce of the Iewes / & accused that Iewe of that whiche he hadde sene in his hous / thenne the Iewes assembleden & cam to the hous of hym / & sawe thymage of Ihesu Cryst / and they took that Iewe and bete hym / & did to hym many iniuryes / & caste hym out half dede of their synagoge / & anone they defowled thymage with their feet / & renewed in it all the tormentes of the passion of oure lorde / & and when they perced his syde with the spere / blood and water yssued haboundauntly / in so moche that they fylled a vessel / whiche they set therunder / And thenne the Iewes were abasshhed & bare this blood in to theyr synagoge & and alle the seke men and malades that were enoynted therwyth / were anone guarysshed & made hool / & thenne the Iewes told & recounted al this thynge by ordre to the bishop of the countre / & alle they with one wyll receyved baptysm in the faythe of Ihesu Cryst / & the bisshop

---

[43] *Invited.*
[46] *Pacified, appeased.*

putt the blood in ampulles[47] of Crystalle & of glas for to be kepte / & thenne he called / the Crysten man that had lefte it in the hows / & enquyred of hym / who had made so fayr an ymage / & he said that Nychodemus had made it / And when he deyde / he lefte it to gamalyel / And Gamalyel to Zachee and Zachee to Iaques / and Iaques to Symon / and hadde ben thus in Ierusalem unto the destruction of the Cyte / and fro thennes hit was borne in to the Royamme of Agryppe of Crysten men / and fro thennes hit was brought ageyne into my countreye / & it was left to me by my parentes by rightful herytage / & this was done in ye yere of our lord seven honderd and fifty / and thenne alle the Iewes hallowed[48] their synagogues in to chirches and therof cometh the custoume that Chirches ben hallowed / For tofore that tyme the aultres were but halowed only / and for this myracle the chirche hath ordeyned / that the fyfte Kalendar of december / or as it is redde in another place / the fyfthe ydus of Novembre shold be the memorye of the passyon of oure lord / wherfor at Rome the chirche is halowed in thonoure of our savyour whereas is kepte an ampulla with the same blood / And there a solempne feste is kepte and done / and there is proved the ryght grete vertue of the crosse unto the paynyms and to the mysbylevyd men in alle thynges /.

And saynt Gregory recordeth in the thirdde booke of his dyalogues / that whanne andrewe Bisshop of the Cyte of Fundane suffred an holy noune to dwelle with him / the fende[49] thenemy beganne temprynte in his herte the beaulte of her / in such wise / that he thought in hys bedde wycked and cursyd thynges / and on a daye a Iewe cam to Rome / and whanne he sawe / that the day fayled / and myghte fynde no lodgynge / he wente that nyght / and abode in the Temple of appolyn /. And bycause he doubted of the sacrylege of the place / how be hit / that he hadde no faythe in the Crosse / yet he markyd and garnysshed hym wyth the signe of the Crosse / then at mydnyght whan he awoke / he sawe a companye of evylle sprytes / whiche went to fore one / like as he hadde

---

[47] *Ampullæ, bottles or flasks.*
[48] *Consecrated.*
[49] *Fiend.*

somme auctoryte puysiance[50] above thother by subiection /
and thenne he sawe hym sytte in the myddes among the
others / and beganne to enquyre the causes and dedes of
everyche[51] of these evylle sprytes / whyche obeyed hym / and
he wold knowe / what evylle everyche had doo / But Gregory
passyth the maner of this vysyon / bycause of shortnes / But
we fynde semblable in the lyf of faders / That as a man entryd
in a Temple of thydolles / he sawe the devylle syttynge / and
all his meyny[52] aboute hym. And one of these wycked /
sprytes cam / and adouryd hym / and he demaunded of hym /
Fro whens comest thow / and he sayd / I have ben in such a
provynce / and have moeved grete warres / and made many
trybulacions and have shedde moche blood / and am come to
telle it to the / and Sathan sayd to hym / in what tyme hath
thow done this / and he sayd in thyrtty dayes and Sathan sayd
/ why hast thow be soo longe there aboutes / and sayd to them
that stode by hym / goo ye and bete hym / and all to lasshe
hym / Thenne cam the second and worsshiped hym / & sayde
Syre I have ben in the see / and have moeved grete wyndes
and tormentes / & drowned many shippes / & slayn many
men / and Sathan sayde how longe hast thow ben aboute thys
/ & he sayd ꝟꝟii dayes / & Sathan sayd hast thou done no
more in this tyme / & commanded that he shold be beten /
and the third cam / & said / I have ben in a Cyte & have
mevyd stryves and debate in a weddynge / and have shed
moche blood / & have slayne the hosbond / & am come to
telle the / & sathan sayd / in what time hast thou done this /
& he said in ten dayes / & he sayd hast thou done no more in
that time / & commanded them that were aboute hym to bete
hym also / Thenne cam the fourth & sayd / I have ben in the
wylderness fourty yere / and have laboured aboute a monke /
& unnethe at the laste I have throwen & made hym falle in
the synne of the flesshe / & when satan herd that / he aroos
fro his sete / & kyssed hym / & tooke hys crowne of his hede
/ & set it on his hede / & made hym to sytte with hym / &
sayde / thou hast done a grete thynge / & hast laboured more

---

[50] *Power.*
[51] *Each or every one.*
[52] *Attendants.*

/ than all thother / and this may be the maner of the vysyon / that saynt gregorye leveth / whan eche had sayd / one sterte up in the myddle of them alle / & seyd he hadde mevid Andrewe ageynste the name / & had mevyd the fourth part of his fleshe agenst her in temptacion / & therto / y[t] yesterday he drough[53] so moche his mynde on her / that in the hour of evensonge he gaf to her in Iapping[54] a busse[55]/ & seid pleynly y[t] she must here it that he wold synne with her / thenne the mayster commanded hym that he shold perform y[t] he had begonne / & for to make hym to synne he shold have a syngular Vyctory and reward among alle the other /. And thenne commaunded he that they shold goo loke who that was that laye in the Temple / And they wente / & loked / And anone they were ware / that he was marked with the signe of the crosse / And they levynge aferd escaped / and sayd / veryly this is an empty vessel / alas / alas / he is marked /. And with[56] thus wys alle the company of the wykked sprytes vanysshed awaye / And thenne the Iewe al amoevyd cam to the bisshop / and told to hym all by ordere what was happend / And whan the bisshoppe herd this / he wept strongly / and made to voyde all the wymmen oute of his hows / And thenne he baptysed the Iewe.

Seynt Gregory reherceth in his dyalogues that a nonne entryd into a gardyne / and sawe a letuse / and coveyted that / and forgate to make the signe of the Crosse / and bote[57] it glotonously / And anone fylle doune and was ravysshed of a devylle / And ther cam to her saint Equycyon[58]/ And the devylle beganne to crye and to saye / What have I doo / I satte uppon a lettuse / and she cam / and bote me / and anone the devylle yssued oute by the commaundement of the holy man of god /. It is redde in thystorye Scolastyke / that the paynyms had peynted on a walle the armes of Serapis / And

---

[53] *Drew.*

[54] *Jest.*

[55] *Kiss.*

[56] *In this wise.*

[57] *Bit.*

[58] St. Equitius was a hermit, and looked after the welfare of other hermits and monks. He took a special interest in a convent of young virgins; died about A.D. 540.

Theodosyen dide doo putt them oute / and made to be paynted in the same place the signe of the Crosse / And when the paynims & priestes of thydolles sawe that / anone they dyde them to be baptysed / sayenge / that it was gyven them to understonde of their olders / that those armes shold endure tyll / that suche a signe were made then / in whiche were lyf / And they have a lettre / of whiche they use / y^t they calle holy / & had a forme that they said it exposed and signyfyed lyf perdurable.

Thus endeth the exaltacion of the holy Crosse.

Having read these extracts from the Golden Legend, we shall be able to understand the accompanying illustrations, which represent some frescos of the fifteenth century, which formerly adorned the walls of the / Chapel of the Gild of the Holy Cross, at Stratford-upon-Avon; which stands close by New Place, Shakespeare's house. These frescos, alas! no longer exist, for, in 1804, the Chapel underwent considerable repair, during which, under the whitewash, were discovered traces of paint, and these, being scraped, a series illustrating the legend of the Cross was found in the chancel, which was built in 1450. In other parts of the Chapel were found representations of the Ressurection, and the day of Judgment, St. George and the Dragon, and the death of St. Thomas a Becket, besides others.

Luckily, a gentleman from London, a Mr. Fisher, was then staying at Stratford-on-Avon, and he drew, and painted them—afterwards, in 1807, publishing them—and it is from his sketches that these illustrations are taken. The barbarians of Stratford hacked the plaster on which the Holy Cross series was painted to bits, and whitewashed all the other paintings. It is presumed they still exist, for, when the Chapel was thoroughly restored in 1835, traces of the other pictures were visible under the whitewash.

These pictures of the Invention, and Exaltation, of the Holy Cross are especially interesting, not only on account of their age and artistic merit, but from the fact that they are of English work, and show the English idea of treating the subject. I have reproduced them all but two; one, the fight on the bridge over the Danube between Heraclius and the son of Chosroes, and the other representing Heraclius smiting off Chosroes' head.

A

Plate **A** represents the visit of the Queen of Sheba to Solomon. Her name was Balkis, and, in her legendary history, it is reported that Solomon, having heard of her riches and power, sent her a peremptory message to submit herself to his rule. She, dreading war with so potent a sovereign, sent an embassy to try and find out whether Solomon was as wise as he was represented to be. With this object she dressed five hundred boys as girls, and a like number of girls as boys, and, among other presents, sent a pearl, a diamond cut through in zigzags, and a crystal box; and she should be able to judge of his wisdom and power, if he could tell the boys from the girls, pierce the pearl, thread the diamond, and fill the goblet with water that came neither from the earth nor the sky.

Needless to say, Solomon passed through the ordeal triumphantly. He ordered silver basins to be brought, so that the ambassadors' suite might wash their hands after their long journey, and the boys were easily distinguished from the girls, for they dipped their hands only in the water, whilst the girls tucked up their sleeves and washed their arms as well as their hands. Then he opened the box containing the pearl, diamond, and goblet, and, taking out the pearl, he applied his magic stone, Samur, or Schamir, which a raven had brought him, and which had the power of cleaving anything, and lo! the pearl was pierced; then he examined the diamond, which was so pierced that no thread could be passed through it; so he took a worm, and having placed a piece of silk in its mouth, it wriggled through, and the diamond was threaded. The next task was to fill the goblet, which he gave to a negro slave, and bade him mount a wild horse and gallop it till it streamed with sweat, and then to fill the goblet with it, thus fulfilling the imposed conditions. He then gave back these presents to the ambassadors, who speedily returned to Queen Balkis. She at once saw that it would be useless to oppose the powerful will of Solomon, and immediately set out on her journey to that monarch.

It is here that her connection with the holy Cross comes in, for its wood, which Solomon had cut down in order to incorporate it into his Temple, and which had the inconvenient property of fitting in nowhere, being either too long or too short for any purpose, was in consequence thrown aside, and ultimately was used as a foot-bridge across a brook. Across this plank the Queen had to pass, but she, recognising its holy virtue, refused to walk across it, preferring to wade the brook, which, having done, she expounded its value to Solomon, and prophesied that out of it should be made the Cross on which Jesus should suffer.

She afterwards became one of Solomon's wives, and bore him a son, and then returned to her own land, and from this son are descended the kings of Abyssynia.

The legend on the label is, as far as is legible, Regina Saba fama Salomonis (adduct) a venit (Iero)soluma ubi lignum in . . . abatica . . . . it . . . gonis . . . persolvetur.

B

Plate **B** is, virtually, two; one showing the angel appearing to Constantine when, early in the fourth century, he was advancing towards Rome against Maxentius; but the legend of the miraculous inscription which appeared in the sky, "In hoc signo vinces," does not appear. The other, and larger portion, represents his victory over Maxentius, and he is represented as spearing and killing that monarch; but this is not historically correct, for, after his defeat, as Maxentius fled towards Rome, essaying to cross the Tiber over a rotten bridge, it gave way, and he was drowned. It is noticeable that the Christian flag bears the Tau Cross.

The Plates **C** *and* **D** *run into each other, although they portray different subjects,* **C** *being the departure of St. Helena for Jerusalem on her quest of the holy Cross. The label in this fresco is utterly illegible.*

Plate **D** shows Judas (called Julius in the label) Cyryacus (the Quyryache of the Golden Legend) being released, after having been forced, through imprisonment and starvation, into confessing where the holy Cross lay buried. In the upper part St. Helena is receiving the holy Cross, whilst labourers are uncovering the Tau Crosses of the two thieves.

The legend is mutilated, but enough remains to make its meaning clear: "Here Seynte helyne examy(neth) the I(ews for) y^e Holy cros . . . . Iulius cyryacus (saith that he knew w)here hete was."

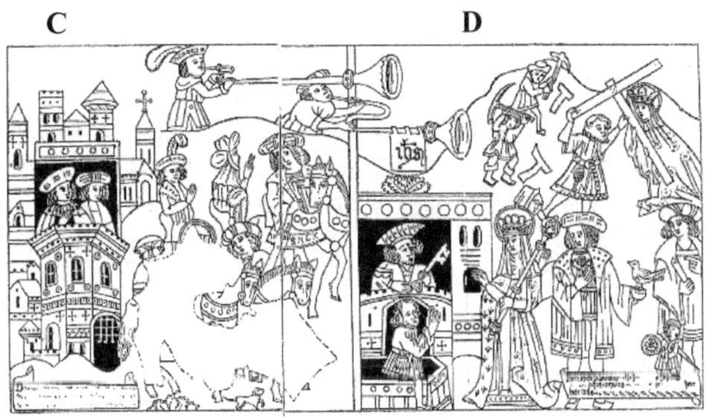

The legend in Plate **E** *is nearly perfect, and accurately describes the painting,* "Hyt was proved evidently by myrakel which was y^e very cros that oure Savyour suffyred . . . . In resynge a made from deth to lyfe."

Here all the Crosses are of the Tau type, and the scene is laid in a forest, where an old labourer, and a bill-man, and the deer nibbling the trees, give a rural aspect, instead of in the

City of Jerusalem, as saith the Golden Legend.

Plate **F** evidently consists of two separate paintings—one, where St. Helena is reverently carrying the Cross into Jerusalem, whilst the angels in heaven are discoursing celestial music; and the other, its reception either in Jerusalem or Byzantium, whither St. Helena sent a portion as a present to her son. And this latter seems the more probable, if we imagine the King, who, with St. Helena, is adoring the Crucifix, to be the emperor Constantine, a fact which might have been settled had the label been legible.

The legend at the bottom is unfortunately mutilated, but that evidently relates to that portion of the Cross which remained at Jerusalem, because it speaks of Chosroes: "Here the hole cros was broughte solemly yn to the . . . in y^e bysshops hands easily and (remaynyd) un to the tyme of (King Codsd)roe.

Plates **G** and **H** represent the story told in the Golden Legend, of Heraclius bearing the Cross into Jerusalem, how the gate miraculously closed, and an angel appeared in the heavens and reproved Heraclius for riding in state on the very spot where Jesus had gone in all meekness, and lowliness, to His passion. The legend is erased in parts, the unmutilated portion reading, "As the nobul kynge eraclyus com rydyng towarde ye cytte of Ierusalem beryng ye crosse so grete pryde . . . where y^e . . . ."

Naturally, the possession of a piece of the true Cross would be esteemed as a most precious property. No matter how small, it would be reverentially enclosed in crystal and gold, and was more than a present fit for an emperor or king, and we cannot marvel that small pieces were distributed all over Christendom. Possibly some of the relics shown as pieces of the very Cross might not have been what they were supposed to be, but it is hard to believe what John Calvin[59] wrote about it:—

"And fyrst of all let us begynne to speake of his crosse, whereupon he was hanged. I know that it is holden for a certaintie that it was founde of Heline the mother of Constantine the Romaine Emperour. I knowe also what certaine Doctours have written touching the approbation hereof, for to certifie that the crosse which she found was without doute the selfe same on the whiche Iesus Christ was hanged. Touchynge all this I reporte me to the thynge it selfe, so much is there that it was but a folish curiositie of her, or at the least a folishe and unconsidered devotion. But yet put the case it had ben a worke worthy of prayse to her, for to have taken paynes to fynde the trewe crosse, and that our lord had then declared by myracle that it was his crosse which she found; Yet let us onely consider that which is of our time. Every one doeth holde that this crosse which Helene founde is yet at Ierusalem, and none doeth doute thereof. Although the Ecclesiasticall history against sayeth the same notablye. For it is ther recited that Helene toke one part thereof to send to the Emperour her sonne, who put the same at Constantinople upon a fyne pyller of Marble in the myddest

---

[59] I quote from the translation by Steven Withers, 1561.

of the market. Of the other part, it is sayde that she did locke the same in a copher of silver, and gave it to the Bishop of Ierusalem to kepe. So then eyther we shall augment the historie of a lie or els that which is holden at this daye of the true Crosse, is but a vayne and triflyng opinion.

"Let us consider on the other part howe many peeces there are thereof throug out the worlde. Yf I would onely recite that whiche I coulde say there woulde be a register sufficient to fyl a whole boke. There is not so little a town where there is not some peece thereof, and that not onelye in cathedrall churches, but also in some parishes. Likewise ther is not so wicked an abbey where there is not of it to be shewed. And in some places ther are good great shydes:[51] as at the holye chappell of Paris, and at Poitiers & at Rome, where there is a great crucifix made thereof as men saye. To be short, yf a man woulde gather together all that hath bene founde of this crosse, there would be inough to fraighte a great ship. The Gospell testifieth that the crosse myght be caried of one man. What audacitie then was this to fyll the earth with pieces of wod in suche quantitie, that thre hundred men can not cary them," &c.

Calvin was full of zeal, and could not stoop to particularise. Witness his assertion that the Cross would freight a ship, and yet that three hundred men could carry it. M. Rohault de Fleury has gone very minutely into this matter. Knowing, from microscopical examination, that several of the relics of the Cross were of pine, he accepts this wood as his basis, and, from its probable size, he deduces a weight of 100 kilogrammes, equal to about 240 English lbs.; and, taking the average density of pine, he estimates that this would give 178 millions of cubic millimetres. He then describes all the known pieces in Europe, Jerusalem, and Mount Athos, with their measurements, and he puts the outcome at 3,941,975 cubic millimetres; thus, according to his shewing, there is but a very small portion of the Holy Cross in existence. I subjoin his list of the places in which pieces of the Cross are known to exist, as it is most interesting, showing the comparative bulk of the pieces, in cubic millimetres:—

Aix la Chapelle	150
Amiens	4,500
Angers	2,640
Angleterre	30,516
Arles	8,000
Arras	10,314
Athos (le Mont)	878,360
Autun	50
Avignon	220
Baugé	104,000
Bernay	375
Besançon	1,000
Bologne	15,000
Bonifacio	47,960
Bordeaux	3,420
Bourbon l'Archambault	29,275
Bourges	22,275
Bruxelles	516,090
Chalmarques	"
Châlons	200
Chamirey	605
Chatillon	"
Cheffes (Anjou)	100
Chelles	"
Compiègne	1,896
Conques	108
Cortone	3,000
Courtrai	200
Dijon	33,091
Donawert	12,000
Faghine	"
Florence	37,640
Fumes	5,250
Gand	436,450
Gênes	26,458

Gramont	5,000
Jancourt (Aube)	3,500
Jerusalem	5,045
Langres	200
Laon	"
Libourne	3,000
Lille	15,112
Limbourg	133,768
Longpont	1,136
Lorris	"
Lyon	1,696
Mâcon	2,000
Maestricht	10,000
Marseille	150
Milan	1,920
Montepulciano	500
Naples	10,000
Nevers	176
Nuremberg	"
Padoue	64
Paris	237,731
Pisa	8,175
Poitiers	870
Pontigny	12,000
Raguse	169,324
Riel les Eaux	671
Rome	537,587
Royaumont	"
Saint Dié	99
Saint Florent	400
Saint Quentin	5,000
Saint Sepolcro	200
Sens	69,545
Sienne	1,680
Tournai	2,000
Trèves	18,000

Troyes	201
Turin	6,500
Venice	445,582
Venloo	”
Walcourt	2,000
Wambach	”
Total	3,941,975

According to this table we are credited in England with 30,516 cubic millimetres of the holy Cross, and it is interesting to know where they are situated. M. Rohault de Fleury, writing in 1870, says there were pieces at Isleworth; St. Gregory, Downside, near Bath; in the possession of Lord Petre; at Bergholt East, in Suffolk; at Plowden; at the convent of St. Mary, York; at West Grinstead; at St. George's, Southwark; and Slindon, Sussex.

These pieces of the holy Cross are not large, as the following table, in cubic millimetres, shows:

At Isleworth	1,000
” College of St. Gregory	6,120
Lord Petre (two relics)	8,287
At St. Mary, Bergholt East	1,008
” Plowden Hall, Salop	262
” St. Mary, York (two relics)	5,600
” West Grinstead ”	38
” St. George's, Southwark (four relics)	63
” St. Richard, Slindon	8,100
Total	30,516

One relic at St. Mary's Convent, York, is very fine; it is ornamented with scroll-work of the tenth century, and bears three impressions of the seal of the Vicar Capitular of the diocese of Saint Omer, 1657 to 1662. It is a pectoral cross that is supposed to have belonged to the patriarch Arnulph, who was with Robert, Duke of Normandy.

The other is supposed to have been attached to the above, and to have belonged equally to Arnulph, patriarch of

Jerusalem. This is kept in a silver reliquary, which also contains relics of SS. Ignatius Loyola and François Xavier.

We see by the Golden Legend, that St. Helena, after finding the Cross, feeling certain that the nails were not far off, prosecuted a further search for them, and they were discovered "shynyng as gold." As with the fashion of the Cross, whether it was *immissa* or *commissa*, there is, and was, a controversy with regard to the nails, whether three or four.

Bosius in his learned and exhaustive book, *Crux Triumphans et Gloriosa*,[60] gives several authorities for three nails only—foremost, Gregory Nazianzen; but he does not give the passage where it may be found; the quotation, however, is

Γυμνὸν τρισήλῳ κείμενον ξύλῳ λαβών

"having taken from the three-nailed wood the dead (or hanging) body." Thus clearly showing the number of nails he considered right.

Bosius then goes on to quote Apollinaris Laodicenus, who, in his tragedy entitled *Christus patiens*, called the holy Cross by the same words, τσισηλον ξυλω, "three-nailed wood"; and he also quotes from the *Meditat. vitæ Christi* of Bonaventura, "*Illi tres clavi sustinent totius corporis pondus.*" Nonnus, the Greek poet, writing in the fifth century, also says that our Lord's feet overlapped each other, and were fastened by only one large nail. So that there is a very fair amount of antiquity in favour of three nails.

Against this theory may be quoted the authority of St. Cyprian, St. Augustine, St. Gregory of Tours, Pope Innocent III., Rufinus, Theodoret, and others, who say four nails were used in the Crucifixion of our Saviour. The battle waged pictorially; but perhaps the earliest known representation of the Crucifixion, that found in the Cemetery of St. Julian, Pope, or of St. Valentine in Via Flaminia at Rome, ought to bear most weight. Our Saviour is represented as being clothed in a long sleeveless robe, which reaches to His ankles; the feet are separate, and are each nailed. It is said that Cimabue was the first to paint the feet overlapping, and one nail. His

---

[60] From this book I have taken the head and tail piece here given.— J. A.

example, however, was much followed, and hence the controversy.

Of these nails, universal tradition says that St. Helena sent two to her son Constantine, and, as the Golden Legend has it, "the emperour dyd do sette them in hys brydel and in hys helme when he wente to batayle." One can understand one of these sacred nails being worn in the Emperour's helmet as a presage of victory and as a safeguard against danger, but the utility of incorporating one of such priceless relics in a horse's bridle is not so easy to comprehend; but the fathers of the Church, St. Cyril of Alexandria, St. Ambrose, Theodoret, and St. Gregory of Tours, recognise in it the fulfilment of the prophecy of Zecharius, chap. xiv. 20: "In that day shall be upon the bridles of the horses, Holiness unto the Lord."

This bridle, or rather bit, is now said to be in existence in France at Carpentras, department of Vaucluse. How it got there is not clearly known, but probably it was taken at the time of the Crusades—as leaden seals on which it is cngraved exist, attached to parchments of the dates 1226 and 1250, and it was mentioned in an inventory of relics in the year 1322.

I have reproduced it, as well as the Iron Crown of Lombardy and the nails, from M. Rohault de Fleury's work, and, as will be seen, it is undoubtedly of great antiquity, closely resembling the bits of the Romans.

According to Bosius, who quotes Gregory Nazianzen, a third nail was thrown by St. Helena into the Adriatic Sea, in order to calm a tempest; and the same authority says that the fourth was deposited in the head of a statue of Constantine, but this militates much against the number of holy nails said to be in existence. Calvin notices this, and is down upon it with sledge-hammer force:—

"Yet there is a greater combat of the nayles. I wyll recite them only that are come to my knowledge. Thereupon there is not so lytle a childe but wyll judge that the Devyll hath to much deluded the worlde in takyng from it both understandyng and reason, that it coulde discerne nothynge in this matter. If the auncient wriiers saye trewe, and namely Theodorile Historiographer of the auncient churche, Helene caused one to be nayled on her sonne's helmet, the other two she put in his horse bitte. How be it Sainct Ambrose sayeth not fully so. For he sayeth that one was put in Constantine's crowne, of the other his horsebit was made, and the thirde Helene kept. Wee se y^t already more than twelve hundred yeres agone this hath bene in controversie, to wit, what was become of the nayles. What certentie can be had of them then at this present time?

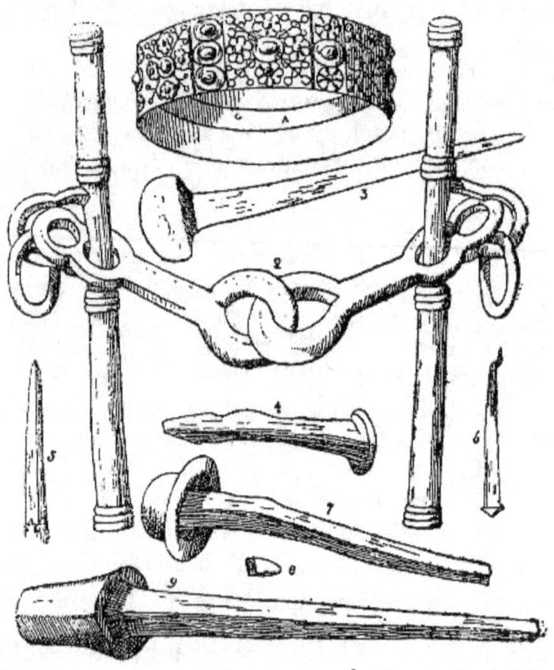

[1] The iron crown of Lombardy. [2] The holy bridle at Carpentras. [3] Nail at Venice. [4] Nail at Rome in Sta. Maria in Campitelli. [5] Nail at Arras. [6] Nail at Colle. [7] Nail in the Church of the Holy Cross of Jerusalem, at Rome. [8] Portion of nail at Toul. [9] Nail at Trèves.

"Now at Millan they boste that thei have y nayle that was put in Constantine's horse bitte. To the whiche the towne of Carpentras opposeth herselfe, sayinge that it is she that hath it. Nowe S. Ambrose doth not saye that the nayle was knit to the bitte, but that the bitte was made thereof. Whiche thynge can in no wyse be made to agre eyther w^t their saying of Milan or w^t theirs of Carpentras.

"Moreover there is one in Rome at Sainct Helenes; another also at Sene, another at Venise. In Germany two: at Collyne one, at the three Maries: another at Triers, one in Fraunce at the holy chappell of Paris, another at ye Carmes, one also at Sainct Denis in France: one at Burges: one at Tenaill, one at Draguine.

"Beholde here fourteene, whereof account is made; in every place they alledge good approbation for themselves, as they suppose. And so it is that everye one hath as good right as aunother. Wherefor there is no better way then to make them all passe under one fidelium. That is to saye, to repute all that they saye hereof to be but lyes, seying that otherwise a man shoulde never come to an ende."

What would Calvin have said if he had seen the formidable list of holy nails enumerated by Guisto (or Justus) Fontanini, Archbishop of Ancyra? which is as follows:—

- 1. Aix la Chapelle.
- 2. Ancona, in the Cathedral.
- 3. Bamberg.
- 4. In Bavaria, Convent of Audechsen.
- 5. Carpentras. The Holy Bit.
- 6. Catania, Sicily.
- 7. Colle, in Tuscany.
- 8. Cologne.
- 9. The Escurial in Spain.
- 10. Milan.
- 11. Monza. The Iron Crown.
- 12. Naples. Monastery of S. Patricius.
- 13. Nuremberg. Church of the Holy Virgin.
- 14. Paris.
- 15. Rome. Two Nails. Church of the Holy Cross of Jerusalem; Church of Santa Maria in Campitelli.
- 16. Sienna. Hospital Sainte Marie de de l'Echelle.
- 17. Spoleto.
- 18. Torcello, near Venice. Church of S. Anthony.

- 19. Torno, on the Lake of Como.
- 20. Toul.
- 21. Trèves.
- 22. Venice. Three nails.
- 23. Vienna.

But this list is further supplemented by M. Rohault de Fleury, who gives six more:—

- 1. Arras, according to M. le Chev. de Linas.
- 2. Compiègne. A point.
- 3. Cracow, in Poland, according to M. Gosselin.
- 4. Florence.
- 5. Lagney.
- 6. Troyes.

So that no less than twenty-nine towns claim the possession of thirty-two nails, all differing in form, the number of which can only be accounted for by the supposition that only a portion of the holy nails has been incorporated into each of them.

THE TITLE OF THE CROSS

One of the most interesting relics in connection with the holy nails is the Iron Crown of Lombardy. This, as may be seen by reference to the illustration (Fig. 1), is a circlet of gold, ornamented with precious stones, and it is indebted for its name of "Iron" to a thin band (**A**) of that metal, which is inside the gold circlet. The Crown itself is of very antique form, being even devoid of rays, and is too small to go on the head. Charlemagne was crowned with it in 774, and Napoleon did not think himself King of Italy until he had placed this precious diadem on his head, in 1805. It is kept at Monza, nine miles from Milan, in the Cathedral, which is of great antiquity. There it reposes in a huge cross placed over the altar.

Of the relics of the Cross there now remains but two specks of the title or inscription thereon, and here, again, I am indebted to M. Rohault de Fleury for the illustration on page xciv., as it seems to me to be the best yet published.

The Evangelists, although agreeing in the spirit of the inscription, vary as to the letter.

Says St. Matthew: "This is Jesus the King of the Jews."

"   St. Mark: "The King of the Jews."

"   St. Luke: "This is the King of the Jews."

"   St. John: "Jesus of Nazareth the King of the Jews."

Neither St. Matthew nor St. Mark note the tri-lingual character, and SS. Luke and John vary as to the order of the different languages; the former saying it was in Greek, Latin, and Hebrew—the latter that it was in Hebrew, Greek, and Latin. The latter is the generally accepted form, and the reason given is, that Hebrew, being the common language, it would naturally come first, as we should do in an English notice, first in English, then, say in French and German, for the benefit of foreigners, as were the Greeks and Romans in Jerusalem.

The tradition is that, along with the Cross, St. Helena found the inscription, and that she sent it, together with a piece of the Holy Cross and a number of other sacred relics, to Rome, where it was deposited in the basilica of Santa Croce. Here it remained until Valentinian, fearing that it might fall into the hands of the Goths and Huns, hid it in the wall of the building, until it was found in 1492.

Valentinian died A.D. 375, and Antoninus Martyr, in his *Do Locis Sanctis* (sec. 20), written about A.D. 570, says he saw the inscription which had been placed on the Cross, and that the words were, "Iesus Nazarenus Rex Iudæorum." He says that he held it in his hand, and kissed it, in the Church of Constantine at *Jerusalem*. Hence it is evident that either tradition is incorrect, or that Antoninus did not tell the truth.

But the claim is that it is, and always has been, in Rome, and Bosius, in his *Crux Triumphans* (p. 60), gives an account of its re-discovery. He says that in February, 1492, Monseigneur Pedro Gonsalvo de Mendoza, Cardinal Sanctæ Crucis, was repairing and cleansing his church, and on the first day of that month, when the workmen reached the top of the arch which was in the middle of the basilica, and near the roof, they saw two small columns; and finding a space, they discovered a niche in which they found a leaden box, well closed, and on its lid was a tablet of marble, on which were engraved these words: Hic est Titvlvs Veræ Crucis. In this box was found a little board, about a hand's breadth and a half, much corroded on one side by time, and bearing, in grooved, engraved characters, which were coloured red, the following inscription: Iesvs Nazarenvs Rex Ivdæorvm. But the word Ivdæorvm was not entire, the last two letters vm having crumbled to pieces by reason of old age. The first line was written in Latin characters, the second in Greek, and the third in Hebrew.

All the city went to see it; and three days afterwards, Pope Innocent went also, and ordered the relic to be preserved in its box, and covered with a sheet of glass. Every one was convinced that they had before their eyes the inscription which Pilate placed upon the Cross over our Saviour's head, and which Saint Helena had deposited in the church at the time of its building.

The relic, as now seen, is very worm-eaten, but the letters are still visible, and have been cut with a small gouge. They read from right to left, as Hebrew does, thus lending great plausibility to the idea that it was done by some Jewish artificers; and it seems to be of some close-grained wood. Taking the piece now at Santa Croce, the whole inscription, if restored, would be thus:

יֵשׁוּעַ וְצַדִּי קוֹלֵךָ הַ׳ יְהוּדִים

IGC RC   NAZAPENRCBAGIAERCIRAGARN

IESVS NAZARINVSRE XINDEORVM

The Inscription at Santa Croce, restored.

NOTES ON THE WOODCUTS

The History of the Legend of the Holy Cross which is here reproduced, is somewhat fuller than the Golden Legend of Caxton, there being particulars about Moses, David, and Solomon not to be found therein; but they may be found in other versions of the Legend, some in the Latin of Jacobus de Voragine, others in two MSS. in the British Museum.[61]

The engravings are taken from a very rare book, of which, as far as is known, there are but three copies in existence: one is in the Royal Library at Brussels, another at the Hague, in the collection of Mr. Schinkel, and the third is in the possession of Lord Spencer at Althorp. It is from this book that these fac-similes (made by M. J. Ph. Berjeau) were taken. The book itself has one woodcut on each page, with a verse in Dutch, at the bottom, explanatory of each engraving. It is called indifferently *Historia Sanctæ Crucis* or *Boec van den houte* (Book of the wood or tree).

It was printed at Kuilenburg on March 6th, 1483, by John Veldener,[62] who had just removed from Louvain. These sixty-four engravings were originally on thirty-two blocks,[63] and

---

[61] Arundel, No. 507, and Add. MSS. 6524.

[62] His life and labours may be read in Mr. Hottrop's *Monuments Typographiques des Pays-bus—*.

[63] See *The Woodcutters of the Netherlands in the 15th Century*, by W. M. Conway, and an article by him in the *Bibliographer* of May,

evidently belonged to some much older block book, now lost. These, Veldener cut in half, as he had already treated a *Speculum*, and brought them out as a fresh book.

The Legend as told by these engravings is as follows:—

ADAM SENDS SETH TO PARADISE FOR SOME OF THE OIL OF MERCY

Adam, feeling himself about to die, sent Seth to Paradise to beg for some of the oil of mercy, which, however, the Archangel Michael refused to give him, but, instead, presented him with three seeds of the tree of life.

1883, p. 32.

THE ARCHANGEL MICHAEL GIVES SETH THREE SEEDS OF THE TREE
OF LIFE

On his return, he found Adam dead, and, being unable to administer these seeds to his father in any other manner, he put them under his tongue, and then buried him.

SETH BURIES ADAM AND PUTS THE THREE SEEDS OF THE TREE OF
LIFE UNDER HIS TONGUE

Presently these seeds germinated and shot through the
ground, and are traditionally said to have been a cedar, a
cypress, and a pine.

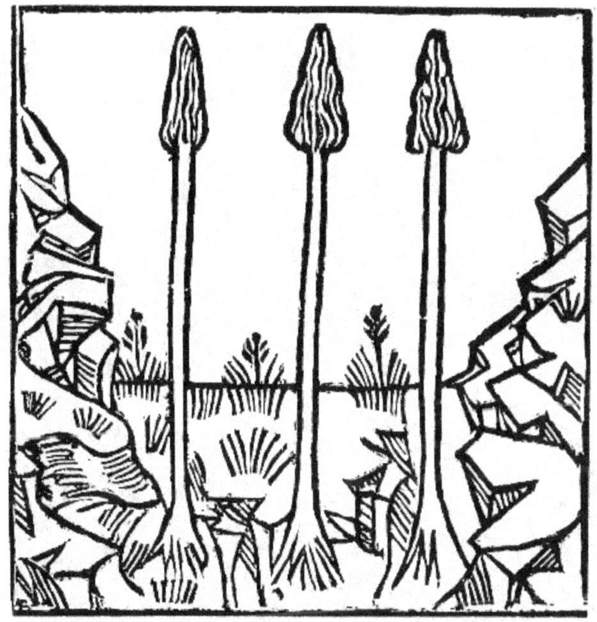

THE THREE SEEDS SPRING UP

They grew until Moses had led the Israelites out of Egypt, when he found them in the Valley of Hebron, and he recognized them as typifying the Trinity. He removed them, and they were his constant companions.

MOSES ALWAYS HAS THE THREE RODS WITH HIM

With them he smote the rock, and the waters gushed out, and the bitter waters of Marah became sweet.

Hier hebben si den beerh hronghevonden
Ende si murmureerden ten seluen stonden
Ende si seyden daer al openbaer
Als dat dat water seer bitter waer

WITH THEM HE MAKES WATER FLOW FROM THE ROCK

AN ANGEL TELLS MOSES HOW TO SWEETEN THE BITTER WATERS

MOSES, BY DIPPING THE RODS IN THE WATERS OF MARAH, SWEETENS
THEM

MOSES PLANTS THE RODS IN THE LAND OF MOAB

He then planted them in the land of Moab, and there they remained, until an angelic vision appeared unto David, and commanded him to go, and take them up, and bring them to Jerusalem.

AN ANGEL APPEARS TO DAVID AND TELLS HIM TO BRING THE RODS TO
JERUSALEM

On his return the three rods worked miracles, healing the
sick, and the leprous, with a touch; nay, more, on being
applied to three black men, they instantly became white.

THE RODS HEAL THE SICK

THE RODS HEAL A LEPER

THE RODS TURN THREE BLACK MEN WHITE

Arrived at Jerusalem, they wished to plant them, but for the night they left them in a cistern, by the Tower of David, and lo! during the night, they struck root, and, entwining themselves, became but one stem, which, when David saw, he had a wall built round it.

DAVID LEAVES THE RODS FOR THE NIGHT

IN THE MORNING HE FINDS THE RODS HAVE TAKEN ROOT AND HAVE
BECOME ONE TREE

DAVID BUILDS A WALL ROUND THE MIRACULOUS TREE

And the tree grew for thirty years, David ornamenting it with rings of sapphire and other precious stones, adding one for every year, and under this tree he composed the Psalms, and praised God exceedingly.

DAVID COMPOSES THE PSALMS AND PRAISES GOD, UNDER THE
SHADOW OF THE TREE

But Solomon, who must needs have all that was rare and
costly to adorn his temple, cast his eyes upon this precious
tree, and ordered it to be cut down.

SOLOMON ORDERS THE TREE TO BE CUT DOWN AND USED IN THE
TEMPLE

It was duly felled, and squared, and trimmed, and it measured
thirty cubits in length.

ARTIFICERS FASHION THE TREE

But when the carpenters came to put it into a place of that length, it was a cubit too short, and when it was fitted into a place of twenty-nine cubits, lo! it measured thirty, and the carpenters marvelled much, and were greatly astonished, and so, being useless, it was laid aside.

THE HOLY WOOD WILL FIT NOWHERE

Yet the people came to see this wonderful tree, and amongst them was a maid named Maximilla, who sat down upon it, and instantly her clothes were in a blaze.

ST. MAXIMILLA SITTING ON THE WOOD, HER CLOTHES CATCH ALIGHT

Then she began to lift up her voice, and prophesy, crying,
"My God, and my Lord Jesu Christ."

Then the Jews took her, and scourged her to death.

ST. MAXIMILLA SCOURGED TO DEATH

The Jews, not knowing what to do with this miraculous tree, laid it across a brook, and, when the Queen of Sheba came to visit Solomon, she recognized the virtue of the wood; and, refusing to defile it with her feet, she dismounted, and adored it, and waded through the brook.

THE WOOD USED AS A FOOT-BRIDGE OVER A BROOK

THE QUEEN OF SHEBA PREFERS WADING THROUGH THE BROOK, TO
WALKING OVER THE HOLY WOOD

Then, when she met Solomon, she reproved him, and told
him that on that tree would the Saviour of the world suffer
death.

THE QUEEN OF SHEBA TELLS SOLOMON OF THE HOLY NATURE OF THE WOOD

And Solomon commanded the holy wood to be taken up, and caused it to be carried into the Temple, there to be placed over the door, so that all men might bless, and adore it, and he coated it over with gold and silver.

THE HOLY WOOD IS TAKEN UP

THE HOLY WOOD IS CARRIED INTO THE TEMPLE

There it remained until Abias stripped it of its costly coverings, and the Jews buried it deep in the earth.

Abias despoils the holy wood of its precious covering

THE JEWS BURY THE HOLY WOOD

There it remained for many years, until the Jews wished to make a pool, where the priests might wash the beasts, to purify them, previous to sacrificing them, and, unknowingly, they dug over the burial-place of the Holy Cross.

DIGGING THE POOL OF BETHESDA

This imparted such a virtue to the water of that pool, which was called Bethesda, that the sick were healed thereat, and an angel at times descended from heaven, and stirred the waters, and then whoever could get first into the waters was straightway healed of any infirmity he might have.

The sick being healed at the Pool of Bethesda

We now come to the Crucifixion, and there was a lack of wood to make Christ's cross—when, suddenly, from the depths of Bethesda, leaped up the tree of the Cross, and floated gently to land. One ran to the High Priest, and told him of the timely find of suitable wood, and he at once gave orders for it to be fashioned into a Cross.

THE HIGH PRIEST TOLD OF THE DISCOVERY OF THE HOLY WOOD

THE HOLY WOOD IS MADE INTO THE CROSS

Then comes the mournful procession to Calvary, with our Saviour fainting under the weight of the Cross, and Simon the Cyrenean is pressed into the service to help Jesus. And then the Crucifixion.

CHRIST BEARING THE CROSS

THE CRUCIFIXION

And whilst the crosses were still standing, the disciples came to them and prayed, and many were healed of their infirmities, and many devils were cast out.

DISCIPLES ADORE THE CROSS, THE SICK ARE HEALED, AND DEVILS
CAST OUT

This so angered the Jews that they took the crosses down, and
buried them, and there they remained until their invention by
St. Helena, A.D. 326. On her arrival at Jerusalem, she
convened a meeting of the principal Jews, and they denied all
knowledge of it, but, on threat of being burnt, they said that

one of their number, named Judas, knew where the crosses were buried.

THE JEWS BURY THE CROSSES

St. Helena comes to Jerusalem

ST. HELENA CALLS TOGETHER THE CHIEF JEWS

Judas, however, refused to tell, and, to compel him to impart
his knowledge, St. Helena had him lowered into a dry well,
"and there tormented hym by hongre and evyl reste."

JUDAS IS PUT INTO A DRY WELL

Seven days of this treatment made him submissive, and at the end of that time he capitulated. He was then drawn up, and prayed to God to direct him to the right spot. His prayer was heard, and after some digging, the crosses were discovered.

JUDAS IS LIBERATED FROM CONFINEMENT

JUDAS PRAYS FOR DIVINE DIRECTION

THE CROSSES ARE DISCOVERED

The news was brought to St. Helena, who visited the spot, but although there were certainly three crosses, no one knew which was the one upon which Jesus suffered. A test, however, was applied, which proved to be satisfactory. The body of a maid was being borne on a bier for burial, but the funeral procession was stopped, and the body was touched by the different crosses.

ST. HELENA VIEWS THE CROSSES

The two first produced no effect, but when the third touched the dead maiden, she was at once restored to life.

TRIAL OF THE TRUE CROSS

A DEAD MAIDEN RAISED TO LIFE BY BEING TOUCHED BY THE TRUE
CROSS

Here, then, was proof positive; this was the very Cross; and
St. Helena, mindful of her son Constantine, divided the
sacred wood; part she enclosed in a case of precious metal,
and kept at Jerusalem; and part she sent to her son, at
Byzantium, who received it with due reverence, and
deposited it in the church, with great ceremony.

ST. HELENA DEPOSITS A PORTION OF THE CROSS IN JERUSALEM

St. Helena gives a portion of the Cross to Constantine

CONSTANTINE DEPOSITS HIS PORTION OF THE CROSS IN BYZANTIUM

Here it remained, until it was taken away, with other spoil, by Chosroes, the King of Persia, who, aware of the sanctity of the relic, had it placed on the right hand of his throne. He was so puffed up with pride, that he ordered himself to be adored. His people, hitherto, had worshipped the sun, but now he ordained that henceforth he was to be considered the principal Person in the Trinity (the Father), and that the relic of the Cross was to be looked upon as the Son, whilst a golden cock which he had made was to represent the Holy Ghost.

CHOSROES COMMANDS HIS PEOPLE TO ADORE HIM

Then Heraclius made war against Chosroes, and meeting with a Persian army under one of the sons of that monarch, it was agreed that, in order to prevent a useless effusion of blood, the two commanders should fight it out between them, and whoever was vanquished should submit.

MEETING OF HERACLIUS AND CHOSROES' SON

The duel was fought on a bridge over the Danube, and Heraclius vanquished and killed the son of Chosroes.

HERACLIUS FIGHTS THE SON OF CHOSROES AND KILLS HIM

The Persian army then made their submission, and the
penance imposed upon them by the conqueror was that they
should all be baptized, which was duly done.

THE PERSIAN ARMY SUBMIT TO HERACLIUS

Heraclius then went to Chosroes, and told him what he had done, offering him his life if he too would embrace Christianity, but the Persian monarch refused, and Heraclius smote off his head.

HERACLIUS VISITS CHOSROES

HERACLIUS KILLS CHOSROES

He then crowned a son of Chosroes, and caused him to be baptized, himself standing sponsor, and buried the slain king with befitting honours.

HERACLIUS CROWNS AND BAPTIZES THE SON OF CHOSROES

BURIAL OF CHOSROES

HERACLIUS TAKES POSSESSION OF THE RELIC OF THE CROSS

Then, taking possession of the holy relic,[64] he set out with it for Jerusalem. But, as he was bearing it in great state, he came to that gate of the City through which Jesus went to His passion, worn, buffeted, scorned, and weary, carrying the heavy burden of His cross. And suddenly the gateway became solid masonry, so that he could not pass through, and

---

[64] *Blocks—billets*

an angel appeared in the heavens, and reproved him for his ostentatious display in a place which his Saviour had previously trodden in such deep humility. Heraclius dismounted from his horse, and, stripping himself of all the trappings of royalty, barefoot, and in his shirt, he meekly bore the Cross to its appointed place, the masonry disappearing as soon as he had humbled himself.

HERACLIUS, ATTEMPTING TO ENTER JERUSALEM, IS MIRACULOUSLY
PREVENTED, AND IS REPROVED BY AN ANGEL

HERACLIUS DIVESTS HIMSELF OF STATE

Heraclius places the relic of the Cross in its appointed place

A piece of the Cross was afterwards sent to Rome, where it duly arrived after a very stormy voyage, and it was there preserved for the adoration of the faithful.

A PORTION OF THE CROSS IS SENT TO ROME, THE VESSEL BEARING IT
MEETING WITH A STORM

THE RELIC OF THE CROSS EXPOSED FOR ADORATION